Sheamus

By Robert Walker

Crabtree Publishing Company

www.crabtreebooks.com

Crabtree Publishing Company
www.crabtreebooks.com

Author: Robert Walker
Publishing plan research and development:
  Sean Charlebois, Reagan Miller
  Crabtree Publishing Company
Coordinating editor: Paul Humphrey
Editorial director: Kathy Middleton
Editors: Clare Hibbert, Crystal Sikkens
Photo researcher: Clare Hibbert
Proofreader: Wendy Scavuzzo
Designer: Ian Winton
Series design: Ken Wright
Production coordinator and
  prepress technician: Samara Parent
Print coordinator: Katherine Berti

Produced for the Crabtree Publishing
Company by Discovery Books

This book is not an official WWE publication.
WWE is not associated, affiliated, or
endorsing the contents of this book.

Photographs:
Alamy Ltd: ZUMA Press, Inc.: page 4;
  Pittsburgh Post-Gazette/ZUMA Wire Service:
  page 12; Allstar Picture Library: page 18;
Corbis: Chris Ryan: pages 9, 24; Dimitri
  Iundt/TempSport: page 22; Matt Roberts/
  ZUMA Press: cover, page 28
Flickr: hisham.omar30: page 5
Getty Images: TIM SLOAN/AFP: page 8;
  Steve Haag/Gallo Images: page 25
Keystone Press: wenn.com: page 14; BIG
  Pictures UK: page 26
Photoshot: EFE: page 16; Sebastian Kahnert/
  Picture Alliance: page 17; Maneesh
  Bakshi/Xinhua: page 19
Shutterstock: Eoghan McNally: page 6; Mircea
  Foto: page 10; ostill: page 11; Helga Esteb:
  page 27
Wikimedia: Anton Jackson: pages 1, 15, 23;
  Mshake3: page 7; Jeremy Jagoda: page 13;
  Shamsuddin Muhammad: page 20;
  simononly: page 21

Library and Archives Canada Cataloguing in Publication

Walker, Robert, 1980-
    Sheamus / Robert Walker.

(Superstars!)
Includes index.
Issued also in electronic format.
ISBN 978-0-7787-8054-0 (bound).--ISBN 978-0-7787-8059-5 (pbk.)

    1. Sheamus, 1978- --Juvenile literature. 2. Wrestlers--Ireland--
Biography--Juvenile literature. 3. Wrestlers--United States--
Biography--Juvenile literature. I. Title. II. Series: Superstars! (St.
Catharines, Ont.)

GV1196.S54W35 2012   j796.812092   C2012-906836-5

Library of Congress Cataloging-in-Publication Data

Walker, Robert, 1980-
    Sheamus / by Robert Walker.
      p. cm. -- (Superstars!)
    Includes index.
    ISBN 978-0-7787-8054-0 (reinforced library binding) -- ISBN
978-0-7787-8059-5 (pbk.) -- ISBN 978-1-4271-9073-4 (electronic (pdf)
-- ISBN 978-1-4271-9127-4 (electronic (html))
    1. Sheamus, 1978---Juvenile literature. 2. Wrestlers--United States--
Biography--Juvenile literature. I. Title.

GV1196.S54W35 2013
796.812092--dc23
[B]
                                            2012040531

Crabtree Publishing Company

www.crabtreebooks.com   1-800-387-7650

Printed in the U.S.A./112012/FA20121012

Published in Canada
Crabtree Publishing
616 Welland Ave.
St. Catharines, ON
L2M 5V6

Published in the United States
Crabtree Publishing
PMB 59051
350 Fifth Avenue, 59th Floor
New York, New York 10118

Published in the United Kingdom
Crabtree Publishing
Maritime House
Basin Road North, Hove
BN41 1WR

Published in Australia
Crabtree Publishing
386 Mt. Alexander Rd.
Ascot Vale (Melbourne)
VIC 3032

CONTENTS

Words that are defined in the glossary are in
bold type the first time they appear in the text.

Meet Sheamus

Imagine yourself as a "wannabe" wrestler, leaping into the ring. Within a split second you have been whirled around in an iron grip, slammed to the mat, and flattened. The roar of the crowd fills your ears.

The Great White

Towering above you is a pale giant of a man with a shock of fiery red hair. They call him the "Great White" or "Celtic Warrior." This is the Irish wrestler Sheamus. He weighs in at 267 pounds (121 kg) and stands 6 feet 4 inches (1.9 m) tall.

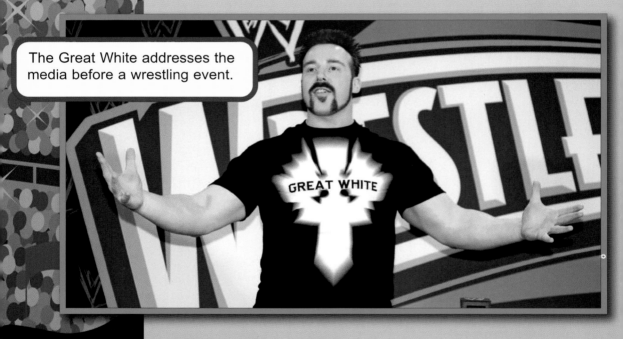

The Great White addresses the media before a wrestling event.

Wrestling Star

Sheamus has been wowing fans since 2002. He hit the big time after signing with the U.S.-based WWE (World Wrestling Entertainment). He was twice WWE Champion (2009, 2010) and U.S. Champion in 2011. In 2012, he won and then successfully defended the WWE World Heavyweight Championship.

Growing Up in Ireland

Sheamus was born on January 28, 1978. His real name is Stephen Farrelly. Today he lives in St. Augustine, Florida, but he was born in Dublin, Ireland. Stephen was raised to be a fluent speaker of the Irish language, Gaelic.

HERO WORSHIP

At school, Stephen learned about Ireland's history and myths that later inspired his wrestling act. He admired the **cunning** hero, Cuchulainn. Stephen has his own emblem that shows a Celtic cross and sword with the word *Laoch*, meaning "warrior" or "hero."

Sheamus wears Celtic crosses to honor his Irish heritage.

Interest in Wrestling

As a child, Stephen watched British and U.S. wrestling. His father Martin, an amateur bodybuilder, brought home videos of WrestleMania contests organized by the WWF (World Wrestling Federation), now called the WWE.

He Said It

I remember when I saw my first wrestling show . . . I didn't sleep for three days afterwards.
—In *The Irish Times*, 2010

5

Tough Sports

Watching wrestling on television is not enough to get you into the ring. Stephen loved playing tough **contact sports**, which was ideal for developing the physical skills he needed as a wrestler.

Gaelic football needs strength, stamina, and flair—just like the WWE contests.

Gaelic Football

One of Stephen's passions was Gaelic football, Ireland's most popular spectator sport. It is a hard, fast game where players carry, pass, bounce, or kick a round ball and try to get it between their opponents' goal posts. Stephen played for Erin's Isle, a club based in Finglas, Dublin.

Rough Rugby

Stephen also played rugby union football for his college. Rugby is similar to football, but played without padding or helmets. This full-contact sport involves running at top speed, pushing and shoving past your opponents, and trying to score a goal by passing or kicking an oval ball.

Ambitions and Dreams

After graduating, Stephen worked as an information technologist, or IT, and a security guard at clubs and arenas, but his dream was to be a professional wrestler. He hit the gym and worked out every day to build up his muscles.

Off to Wrestling School

The Canadian wrestler Bret "The Hitman" Hart suggested that Stephen take a course at the Monster Factory. This popular pro-wrestling school in Paulsboro, New Jersey, had been founded in 1983 by "Nature Boy" Buddy Rogers and "Pretty Boy" Larry Sharpe.

The Monster Factory's long line of famous former students includes the gigantic "Big Show."

Learning the Ropes

Stephen started at the Monster Factory in April 2002. He trained under Larry Sharpe and referee Jim Molinaux. The program was a challenge—a world away from the team sports Stephen had enjoyed back home. He was taught every technical trick that a wrestler needs to know, from rope moves and falls to **submission holds** and aerial stunts.

Two wrestlers practice in the training ring at the Monster Factory, New Jersey.

FIRST NAMES

Stephen's first "character name" was Sheamus O'Shaunessy, or "S.O.S." for short. He also earned the nickname "the Irish Curse," after an illegal low blow to an opponent.

Appearance Matters

Stephen learned how to make a contest look as terrifying and violent as possible—without seriously injuring himself or his opponent. He also discovered he needed a character— someone the crowds would love to boo or cheer. After only six weeks, Stephen had his first match, against the wrestler Robert Pigeon.

Injury Time

Stephen was all set to launch his career as Sheamus O'Shaunessy when he fell during a **hip toss**, injuring his neck. Even though fights are carefully staged, it is all too easy to get badly hurt. Stephen was forced to give up competing for almost two years.

Re-entry in Europe

Sheamus relaunched his career in May 2004, joining up with a new Dublin-based school and promotion team called Irish Whip Wrestling (IWW). He threw himself into a punishing series of individual contests and **tag** events. In 2005, Sheamus was twice winner of the IWW International Heavyweight Championship.

WHAT WHIPS?

Despite the name, IWW contestants did not fight with whips. An Irish Whip is a wrestling move, also known as the Hammer Throw, that involves swinging an opponent into the ropes or corners.

The toughest opponent Sheamus faced at this time was Scottish wrestler Drew Galloway (later McIntyre), shown here pummeling John Cena in 2010.

9

At the Gym

A successful wrestler is part athlete, part bodybuilder, and part actor. He or she must follow a muscle-building diet and work out at the gym to stay fit, agile, and strong. A lot goes into feeding and building a body fit for the ring. When time allows, Sheamus trains five days a week, working on both his upper and lower body strength.

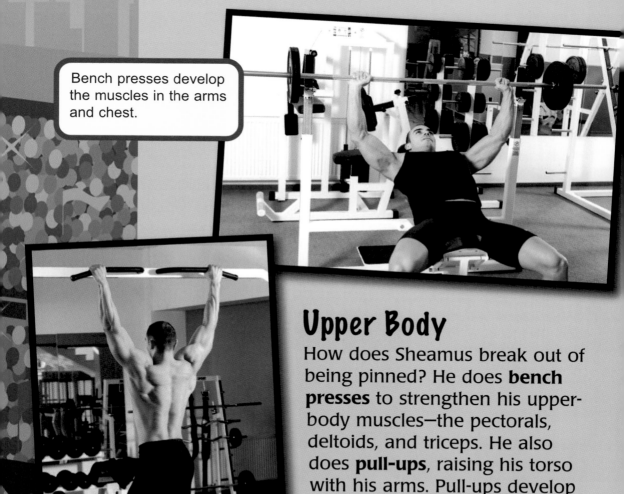

Bench presses develop the muscles in the arms and chest.

Upper Body

How does Sheamus break out of being pinned? He does **bench presses** to strengthen his upper-body muscles—the pectorals, deltoids, and triceps. He also does **pull-ups**, raising his torso with his arms. Pull-ups develop the large back muscles that Sheamus needs for his famous finishing move, the High Cross.

Pull-ups build strength in the back.

Stomach and Legs

You may not know it, but you use your abdominal or stomach muscles for lifting, pushing, and pulling. Sit-ups help Sheamus keep his abdominal muscles tight and strong. He exercises his legs with lower body exercises called lunges. His leg muscles need to be tough and flexible for the powerful high kick he calls the Brogue Kick.

WATCH OUT!

Exercising without supervision is dangerous. Sheamus follows carefully planned exercise programs that are tailored for his fitness level and ability.

Lunges seriously stretch the leg muscles.

On the Rise

In November 2006 and April 2007, Sheamus had tryout matches for WWE. It was after these tryouts that he finally got the call he wanted. WWE was offering Sheamus a huge opportunity, so he wasted no time thinking about it. He caught the first flight to the United States.

Off to Tampa

Sheamus signed up to a **development contract**. This meant that he was part of a WWE **franchise**, but would first gain experience on one of two smaller wrestling circuits. His destination? Florida—soon to be WWE's only development territory.

Ex-wrestler Steve Keirn, who often performed as Doink the Clown, ran WWE's development territory in Tampa, Florida.

Fighting in Florida

Sheamus had to adjust to the climate in his new home. Florida is subtropical—very hot and humid. This was a big change from the cool, rainy cities of Britain and Ireland, but Sheamus had a career to build.

Sheamus uses an armbar hold on Eric Escobar during an FCW bout.

PALE FACE

Fair-skinned Sheamus burns easily in the sunlight. Unable to get a fashionable tan, he has made his chalky-white complexion a part of his image in the ring.

In Development

In October 2007, Sheamus began a two-year stint with Florida Championship Wrestling (FCW, the predecessor of today's NXT Wrestling). He wrestled with tag teams and in singles competitions, and briefly reigned as Florida Heavyweight Champion. During this time, Sheamus learned to be stronger and faster in the ring and worked up his persona, the Celtic Warrior.

Signature Moves

What makes a wrestler stand out from the others? There is of course the attitude, the entrance music, the costume, and the wrestler's treatment of the referee and spectators. Most important of all are those attacking maneuvers that serve as an individual trademark. These are called **signature moves**.

Sheamus demonstrates his signature Repeated Forearm Clubs on wrestler Daniel Bryan.

The War Sword

One classic wrestling move is the Double Axe Handle. For Sheamus, it has another name—the War Sword. He grips both hands together and swings his arms round as if he is on a battlefield, striking his opponent on the chest, neck, or back. Beware of the Celtic Warrior!

He Said It

When I get in there I hit as hard as I can and I let the fella in there know that he's in a fight and...it's not going to be an easy night for him.
—Interview on RTÉ's *The Late Late Show*, April 2011

Rock and Roll

The Rolling Fireman Carry slam is another favorite with Sheamus. First he hauls his opponent over his shoulders, the way a firefighter is trained to lift a body. Over comes one arm and one thigh. With a rush forward he then tips his opponent over and slams him down flat on his back.

The Hard Shoulder

One move that has Sheamus written all over it is the Diving Shoulder Block. Sheamus drops down onto his opponent from above and uses his shoulder to deliver a blow to the upper body. The force of gravity brings him down like a ton of bricks.

Sheamus performs his Diving Shoulder Block move, which is also known as the Battering Ram.

Break Out!

In 2009, Sheamus dropped the O'Shaunessy from his name. Now, as simply Sheamus, he began to play up his role as the villain. He developed rivalries and **feuds** with other leading wrestlers and had a good run of wins.

Big Break

Thanks to WWE's TV **brand shows**, including *ECW*, *SmackDown*, and *Raw*, Sheamus became a big media personality. It was on *Raw* that Sheamus achieved a breakthrough. He won a battle royal. This is a contest in which many wrestlers take to the ring and fight until only one is left as winner. On this occasion, the prize was the chance to **break out** and challenge the reigning champion.

Sheamus takes on fellow-WWE wrestlers Alberto Del Río and Daniel Bryan on *SmackDown*.

Hitting the Big Time

The WWE champ at the time was John Cena, a wrestler with many successes to his name, and also a rap star and actor. Despite Sheamus's ability and larger size, few people thought that he had a chance against the more experienced American.

Challenging the Champ

The championship bid was held December 13, 2009, at the AT&T Center in San Antonio, Texas. It was part of a seven-match extravaganza featuring the stars of WWE's TV shows, and was the first **TLC** match. TLC is a crazy, now annual, event in which tables, ladders, and chairs can be used as legitimate weapons during the pay-per-view televised fight.

The American wrestler John Cena is photographed in London, UK, in 2012.

17

Taking the Belt

The Sheamus versus John Cena bout was a "table match." In order to win, the wrestler had to slam his opponent through a table! Things looked glum for the Irishman. Even the fight announcers doubted his chances. Sheamus did his best to look confident as he entered the ring, but the crowd was chanting for Cena.

The Fight Begins

The reigning WWE champ opened things up with a shot to the face, then charged Sheamus into several turnbuckles (the eyelets attaching the ropes to the posts of the ring). Sheamus broke the pummeling with a shoulder to Cena's face. He followed this up with a **piledriver**, turning his opponent upside down and dropping him to the mat. Then he threw a barrage of punches and a devastating knee slam.

As reigning WWE champ, Cena had everything to lose.

Surprise Ending

The epic struggle continued for almost 10 minutes, with each wrestler in turn gaining and then losing the upper hand. By the time Cena managed to get a table into the ring, both were near exhaustion. Cena prepared to slam Sheamus through the table but, at the last moment, it was Sheamus who threw Cena from the ropes. The table splintered and Sheamus held up to the stunned crowd the coveted belt of a WWE champion.

Sheamus shows off his title belt during a press conference.

He Said It

When I won my first title, people were very jealous, even a lot of the WWE Superstars. There's a saying you've got to pay your dues first, but as far as I'm concerned, paying your dues is an excuse for people who fail to be successful.

—Interview with children's newspaper *First News*, 2010

The Champion

Sheamus was now on a roll as a top star on the main WWE circuit. He proved he was capable of taking on the best, from John Cena to the likes of Triple H and Randy Orton.

King of the Ring

The year 2010 saw a second WWE championship reign for Sheamus. Then, in Philadelphia's Wells Fargo Center, the Celtic Warrior went royal—he won the King of the Ring **elimination tournament**. In March 2011, he added the WWE United States Championship in St Louis, Missouri, to his growing list of achievements.

Sharklike Sheamus

They say that a great white shark never stops swimming. Sheamus, too, has stamina—not only for the fighting but also the endless touring, training, and promotion that make up the life of a pro wrestler. He is on the move four or five days every week, touring across Europe as well as the United States.

King of the Ring Sheamus puts on his crown and royal robes in 2010, after his victory in Philadelphia.

Heavyweight Boss

In January 2012, Sheamus returned to St Louis. There, he won the WWE Royal Rumble, a grueling elimination contest in which multiple combatants enter the ring at different intervals.

The Celtic Warrior wins the World Heavyweight title in April 2012.

Defeating the Dragon

In April 2012, Sheamus took part in WrestleMania XXVIII in Miami Gardens, Florida. He won a place in the record books by defeating World Heavyweight Champion Daniel Bryan, "The American Dragon," in 18 seconds flat! He successfully defended his title that August in Los Angeles, in an electric contest with "The Mexican Aristocrat" Alberto Del Río.

Finishing Moves

To win a bout conclusively, wrestlers rely on a series of final moves called **finishers**. These techniques may involve pinning an opponent to the mat for a count of three—but they can also be used to make an opponent **tap out**, or submit, meaning they have given up.

The standard pinning of an opponent has the victor on top with the loser held down with both shoulders flat on the mat.

He Said It

We're up there knocking lumps out of each other. If the crowd isn't buying it, it doesn't work. You make things happen on the fly. That's what results in a great match.
—In the *Irish Independent*, April 2012

Major Moves

Sheamus developed his amazing High Cross move, also called the Running Crucifix **Powerbomb**, during his years in Florida. Sheamus hoists his opponent over his shoulder, holds their arms out to the sides like a cross, then slams the wrestler into the mat.

Sheamus performs his famous finisher, the High Cross.

High Kick

Another favorite from the Florida ring, the Brogue Kick, is a high-placed kick with 267 pounds (121 kg) of Sheamus packed behind it! A brogue is a strong leather outdoor shoe or a strong Irish or Scottish accent.

Superior Slams

Lower back, beware! For his Irish Curse slam, Sheamus lifts his opponent into the air, throws his victim down onto his knee, then onto the mat. Few wrestlers find their feet after getting this treatment. To set up his White Noise slam, Sheamus has to wrap his opponent over his shoulder. He then jumps and turns, slamming the other wrestler onto their belly on the mat below.

23

Heroes and Villains

With his pale skin and his shock of red hair, Sheamus presents a dramatic public image. Acting, showmanship, and marketing are all very much a part of pro wrestling. The WWE weaves a rich storyline that involves all the wrestlers in the league. There are rivalries, alliances, double-crosses, and side-switches.

Sworn Enemies

Feuds are played out inside the ring as well as outside it. Internet surfers can watch videos of warring parties taunting and cheating one another. These exchanges help to fuel excitement for that moment when opponents meet in the center square.

He Said It

When you walk out there in front of 80,000 people the noise and atmosphere hits you all at once . . . It's the best feeling in the world.
—Interview on Sky Sports, February 2012

Sheamus and Triple H stare each other down in the ring.

Heels versus . . .

A heel is a wrestler who plays the bad guy. He cheats in the ring and breaks the rules. He may be mean or vain, and he sneers at the world. The worse his manners become, the more he entertains the booing crowd.

CHANGING ROLE

Sheamus started out in the WWE as a heel, but from summer 2011 showed a change of heart, appearing in the ring as a face. Mind you, he can still come across as pretty mean when he wants to!

. . . Faces

A face is one of the good guys, who asks for the crowd's sympathy. He himself plays fair, so he pretends to be shocked and dismayed by the treachery and foul play of the heel. Of course, these roles can be switched and alliances made, just to make the plot even more complicated. Sometimes it is all an act, but very often the rivals' anger and needling are real!

Sheamus looks serious enough as he leaps toward the Big Red Monster Kane—but is it all an act?

Sheamus on Screen

Sheamus first appeared on television as a schoolboy, singing in a choir. It's difficult to picture the Sheamus of today as a choirboy! As an adult, his acting talents have kept him almost as busy outside the wrestling ring as in it.

Making Movies

In 2008, Sheamus acted in *The Escapist*, a film set inside a men's prison. He played Two Ton, a thug and bare-knuckle fighter. In 2009, Sheamus had a small part as a prison guard in *3 Crosses*. He also had a role in an Irish horror film, *Legend of the Bog*.

In *Legend of the Bog*, Sheamus plays a Celtic warrior who emerges from a peat bog after thousands of years.

WHAT A MUPPET!

Sheamus has appeared alongside puppets on several Irish television shows. In 2011, he won a Slammy Award for Outstanding Achievement in Muppet Resemblance. The muppet in question? Carrot-topped Beaker!

Stomp Out Bullying!

In real life, Sheamus is one of the good guys. He signed up to the WWE/Creative Coalition's "Don't be a bully—be a STAR!" campaign. "STAR" stands for **S**how **T**olerance **A**nd **R**espect.

Back to School

Sheamus goes into schools to tell the children that bullying must stop. He is popular and always raises a smile. Pupils are often surprised to hear the big muscle man say that he was picked on when he was a small, chubby kid. He knows what being bullied is like.

Sheamus is photographed at a "be a STAR" event in August 2011.

He Said It

It's important for people to realize that bullying isn't cool . . . it's important kids come together and say this is not going to be tolerated. There's strength in numbers.
—Interview in the *The Huffington Post*, August 2011

27

The Dream Goes On

The story of Sheamus is just getting started. When asked about his future plans, he says he tries to be successful by living one week at a time. His main focus is on his career as a wrestler. He's open to doing more movies if the timing is right, but his main priority is with the WWE. He hopes to be able to take on WWE wrestler The Undertaker at WrestleMania XXIX in 2013 or WrestleMania XXX in 2014. Whatever the future holds for Sheamus, whether it's in the ring or on the big screen, you can be sure he'll be entertaining fans.

Sheamus is shown here wearing his WWE U.S. Champion belt in 2011.

Timeline

1978: Sheamus is born Stephen Farrelly in Dublin, Ireland, on January 28

1980s–90s: Stephen is educated at Irish-language schools in Dublin

1990s: Stephen plays Gaelic football for Erin's Isle, Dublin; He studies management at the National College of Ireland

2002: Stephen trains at the Monster Factory in New Jersey, USA; He takes the name Sheamus O'Shaunessy but sustains a neck injury

2004: Sheamus resumes wrestling, signing up with Irish Whip Wrestling (IWW)

2005: Sheamus becomes two-time winner of the IWW International Heavyweight Championship

2006: He competes in Britain with Celtic Wrestling, LDN Wrestling, and All Star Wrestling

2007: Sheamus signs a development contract with World Wrestling Entertainment (WWE) and moves to the United States; He fights with Florida Championship Wrestling (FCW)

2008: Sheamus wins the Florida Heavyweight Championship

2008: He appears in the movie *The Escapist*

2009: Sheamus drops "O'Shaunessy" from his name; In December, he wins the WWE Championship and joins the WWE star circuit

2010: Sheamus wins a second WWE Championship and the King of the Ring tournament

2011: Sheamus takes the WWE United States Championship. He joins the "be a STAR" campaign against bullying

2012: Sheamus defeats Daniel Bryan in just 18 seconds to become World Heavyweight Champion; He successfully defends this title against Alberto Del Río in August

Glossary

bench press An exercise that builds chest and arm muscles through lifting weights on a bar

brand show A TV show featuring wrestlers who are marketed to the public as a group or "brand"

break out Take part in a contest where the prize is the right to take on a reigning champion

contact sport A sport that involves direct physical contact between players, for example football

cunning Clever and crafty

development contract An agreement with a new wrestler to give him experience

elimination tournament A contest in which defeated wrestlers fall out until one winner remains

feud A long-standing dispute

finisher Any move that will end a wrestling bout

franchise A small organization that operates as part of a larger company.

hip toss A move in which a wrestler hooks his arm under his opponent's armpit and throws him

piledriver A move where a wrestler turns his opponent upside down and drives him into the mat

powerbomb A move where a wrestler slams his opponent back-first into the mat

pull-up An exercise that builds back muscles through pulling the body up to a bar

signature move A wrestling move associated with a particular wrestler

submission hold Any hold that forces an opponent to submit (admit defeat)

tag Team wrestling, in which one team member fights until replaced by touching hands with a team member

tap out To tap the mat to indicate a submission

TLC A wrestling contest in which **T**ables, **L**adders, and **C**hairs may be used as weapons

Find Out More

Books

Black, Jake. *The Ultimate Guide to WWE*. New York: Grosset & Dunlap, 2011.

Dinzeo, Paul. *Sheamus* (Pro Wrestling Champions). Minneapolis, MN: Bellwether Media, 2012.

Shields, Brian, and Kevin Sullivan. *WWE Encyclopedia* (Second Edition). New York: Dorling Kindersley, 2012.

WWE Annual 2013. Torquay, UK: Century Books Ltd, 2012.

DVDs

WWE: Royal Rumble 2012
World Wrestling, 2012.

Websites

WWE: Sheamus
www.wwe.com/superstars/sheamus/
The official profile from the WWE website

Sheamus on Facebook
www.facebook.com/pages/Sheamus-WWE-Universe/139548194814
Video playlists, photos, and match results

"be a STAR" website
www.beastaralliance.org/
The anti-bullying campaign that Sheamus supports

Twitter

Follow Sheamus on Twitter
@WWESheamus

Index

About the Author
Robert Walker is an author of popular educational books for young readers. He enjoys spending time with his wife and small dogs.